T0379723

Learn About

THE FIVE SENSES

Tasting

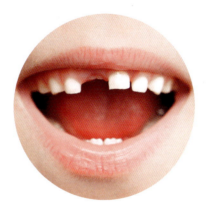

by Claire Caprioli

Children's Press®
An imprint of Scholastic Inc.

Special thanks to our medical content consultant, An Huang, MD, PhD, professor of physiology, New York Medical College.

Library of Congress Cataloging-in-Publication Data
Names: Caprioli, Claire, author.
Title: Tasting / by Claire Caprioli.
Description: First edition. | New York, NY: Children's Press, an imprint of Scholastic Inc., 2024. | Series: Learn about: the five senses | Includes bibliographical references and index. | Audience: Ages 5–7. | Audience: Grades K–I. | Summary: "How do we experience the world? Let's learn all about the five senses! The sense of taste is one of our five senses. And it is amazing! Among many other things, it makes us enjoy food and recognize many different flavors, such as sweet, sour, and salty. In turn, it encourages us to eat and helps us keep strong and healthy. Learn about tasting, how it works, and common problems and diseases connected with it, with this perfect first introduction to the sense of taste! ABOUT THE SERIES: The human body is amazing! It gives us five different ways to learn about the world around us: through the eyes, through the skin, through the tongue, through the ears, and through the nose. Thanks to these parts of our bodies, we can see, feel, taste, hear, and smell. These are the five senses! Why do bananas taste so good? Why does tickling cause so much laughter? Illustrated with familiar examples, this fun nonfiction set in the Learn About series gives readers a close-up look at the five senses, and it teaches them how each of the senses work."— Provided by publisher.
Identifiers: LCCN 2022056745 (print) | LCCN 2022056746 (ebook) | ISBN 9781338898200 (library binding) | ISBN 9781338898217 (paperback) | ISBN 9781338898224 (ebook)
Subjects: LCSH: Taste—Juvenile literature. | Tongue—Juvenile literature. | Senses and sensation—Juvenile literature. | BISAC: JUVENILE NONFICTION / Concepts / Senses & Sensation | JUVENILE NONFICTION / General
Classification: LCC QP456 .C35 2024 (print) | LCC QP456 (ebook) | DDC 612.8/7—dc23/eng/20230124
LC record available at https://lccn.loc.gov/2022056745
LC ebook record available at https://lccn.loc.gov/2022056746

10 9 8 7 6 5 4 3 2 1   24 25 26 27 28

Printed in China, 62
First edition, 2024

Book design by Kathleen Petelinsek

Photos ©: cover, 1: Flavio Coelho/Getty Images; 4–5: kali9/Getty Images; 7 top: Alina555/Getty Images; 7 bottom: Motortion/Getty Images; 8 left: dcdr/Getty Images; 8 center: Svitlana Romadina/Getty Images; 9 right: Lew Robertson/Getty Images; 10: Korovin/Getty Images; 11: Jose Luis Pelaez Inc/Getty Images; 17: BSIP/Getty Images; 19: tylim/Getty Images; 20: gurinaleksandr/Getty Images; 23: didesign021/Getty Images; 26 top: Khosrork/Getty Images; 28 top: David Pillow/Dreamstime; 28 center: Ben Hong/EyeEm/Getty Images; 28 bottom: SCIEPRO/Getty Images; 29 top: Alf Jacob Nilsen/500px/Getty Images; 29 center: J Esteban Berrio/Getty Images; 29 bottom: ANDREYGUDKOV/Getty Images; 30 top left: wilpunt/Getty Images; 30 top right: IL21/Getty Images; 30 bottom left: Waynerd/Getty Images; 30 bottom right: Jose Luis Pelaez Inc/Getty Images.

All other photos © Shutterstock.

TABLE OF CONTENTS

Delicious!

Have you ever eaten a popsicle? It is fruity, sweet, and cold. It can also be a bit sour. It is delicious! You know what you are eating thanks to your sense of taste.

Taste is one of our five senses. The other four are hearing, sight, smell, and touch. The five senses help us take in information about the world around us.

These children are enjoying a sweet treat on a hot day.

CHAPTER I

Our Amazing Taste

Our tongue is what tells us the most about how something tastes. However, when we eat, we don't only use our tongue. We also use our teeth, lips, and mouth. They all give us clues about what we are eating. How a food feels in our mouth helps us recognize it and taste it. Some foods are hard, and some are soft, crunchy, chewy, mushy, or even sticky. Think about a fresh apple and oatmeal. They taste and feel very different!

An apple
is crunchy
and sweet.

Oatmeal
is soft
and mushy.

There are five basic tastes. They are sweet, sour, salty, bitter, and **savory** (also called umami [oo-MAH-mee]). Sweet foods contain sugar. Bananas, grapes, and candy are sweet. Sour foods contain acid. They taste sharp. Lemons and vinegar are sour.

Umami is a Japanese word. It means "pleasant savory taste."

Sweet

Sour

Salty

Salt is a **mineral**. We add salt to food for flavor. Soups and pretzels can be salty. Bitter foods taste harsh. Kale and coffee are bitter. Savory is a rich or meaty taste found in meats and cheeses.

Salt is an important nutrient. However, too much of it is not good for you.

Bitter

Savory or umami

Taste and smell work together. Our sense of smell helps us taste flavors. Have you noticed that food doesn't taste the same when you have a stuffy nose? It is because you can't smell it! Pinch your nose. Eat something with a strong smell like popcorn. It doesn't taste as good!

You can't smell much of anything with a cold! You are also less able to taste.

The pizza is hot and savory. The lemonade is cold, sweet, *and* tart. Tart is another word for sour.

Sweet, sour, salty, bitter, and savory mix in different ways. This creates many flavors. Our sense of smell adds to flavor, too. But that's not all! Our tongue also knows if something is hot, cold, or spicy. In total, humans can taste more than 10,000 flavors!

Spices such as cinnamon and oregano can add a lot of flavor to our food.

CHAPTER 2

Tongue at Work

When we chew, food mixes with **saliva**. Then the food goes all over our tongue. There are tiny bumps on our tongue. The bumps hold **taste buds**. The taste buds send messages to the **nerves**. Nerves tell our brain how something tastes!

The average human tongue is about 3 inches (8 cm) long!

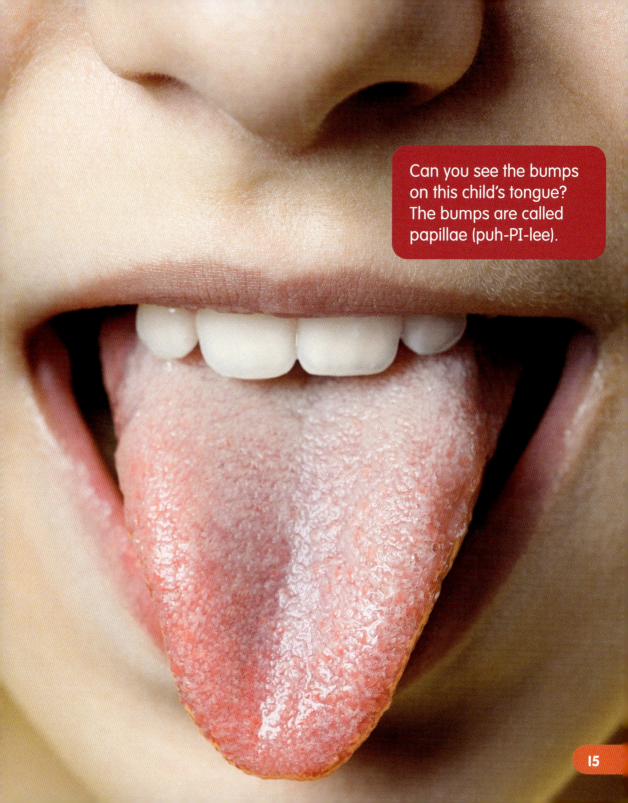

Can you see the bumps on this child's tongue? The bumps are called papillae (puh-PI-lee).

A healthy tongue is bumpy, pink, and wet. Check out its main parts and how it connects to the brain:

PAPILLAE: These are the raised bumps on the surface of the tongue. They contain the taste buds.

TASTE BUDS: They sense if something is sweet, sour, salty, bitter, or savory.

Your taste buds get worn out after a week or two. Then your body replaces them with new ones!

APEX: This is the tip of the tongue.

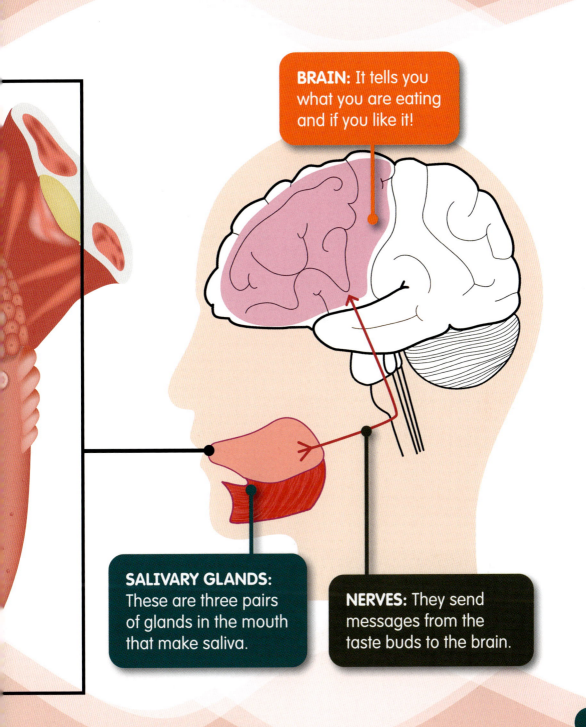

BRAIN: It tells you what you are eating and if you like it!

SALIVARY GLANDS: These are three pairs of glands in the mouth that make saliva.

NERVES: They send messages from the taste buds to the brain.

We have about 10,000 taste buds! The tongue has 9,000 of them. The rest are inside our cheeks, on the roof of our mouth, and in our throat. Our taste buds can help keep us safe. They tell us if food is **spoiled**. Eating spoiled food can make us sick. Some foods taste sour when they have spoiled.

Chickens only have 24 taste buds! Maybe that is why they eat just about anything!

Sour milk tastes gross! Your brain tells you to spit it out!

19

This dog is making lots of saliva! It shows the dog is very hungry.

We need saliva to taste food. Taste buds work better when they are wet. Wet food enters our taste buds for us to taste. There's always some saliva in our mouth. Saliva keeps our mouth moist and healthy. We make even more saliva while eating and drinking.

Humans create more than 4 cups (2 pints) of saliva every day!

CHAPTER 3

Taste Troubles

Sometimes, when we are sick, our sense of taste can change. Foods may not taste the same. But most of the time, once we feel better, our taste recovers. Sometimes a bump on our tongue can become red and painful. This can happen, for example, when we burn or bite our tongue. It should heal on its own within a few days. Then we can go back to enjoying our tasty food!

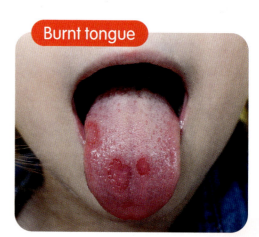

Burnt tongue

Sometimes we need to see a special doctor for the sense of taste. This doctor is called an ear, nose, and throat (ENT) doctor.

Our doctor will know if we need medicine.

Sharing a meal can be a lot of fun!

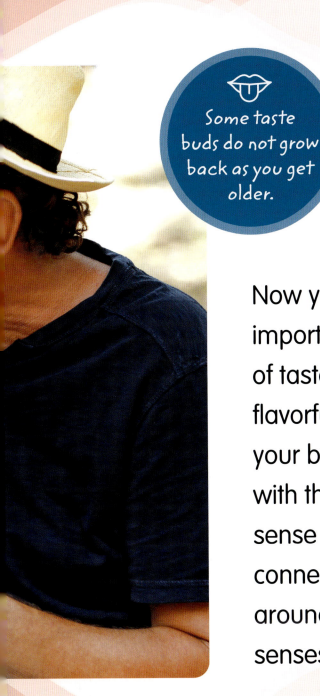

Some taste buds do not grow back as you get older.

Now you know the importance of your sense of taste. It helps you enjoy flavorful foods that keep your body strong. Together with the other senses, our sense of taste keeps us connected with the world around us. What will your senses help you do today?

ACTIVITY: SUPER SALIVA

Discover the power of saliva with this tasty activity. You only need a few things to carry it out!

YOU WILL NEED:

- Clean paper towel
- Teaspoon
- Honey (or maple syrup, brown sugar, or white sugar)

STEPS:

1 Stick out your tongue a comfortable amount.

2 Use a paper towel to dry off your tongue.

3 Add a drop of honey on your dry tongue. Wait 5 seconds. What is your sense of taste telling you?

4 Stick your tongue back in your mouth. Saliva will mix with the honey. What is your sense of taste telling you now? How is it different?

WHAT HAPPENED?

You need saliva to taste food. When your tongue was dry, it was hard to taste. However, when you put your tongue back in your mouth, your saliva mixed with the food and helped it enter your taste buds. Then, the taste buds sent a message to your brain, that was able to tell what you were tasting.

ANIMAL TASTE

Giant Anteater

The Longest Tongue

Giant anteaters have tongues 2 feet (0.6 m) long! They don't have any teeth. They eat a lot of ants! They can eat as many as 30,000 ants in one day. The giant anteater pulls out its long tongue. The ants stick to the anteater's saliva and . . . slurp! The ants are eaten up!

Catfish

Most Taste Buds

Catfish have as many as 270,000 taste buds! But they are not in their mouths. They are all over the outside of their body. Catfish feed along the bottom of the water and eat small fish, clams, seagrass, and insects.

Blue Whale

Heaviest Tongue

A blue whale's tongue can weigh up to 5,400 pounds (2,450 kg). That's as much as an elephant or a car! What do they eat? They mostly eat small krill, which look like shrimp. The blue whale can eat 12,000 pounds (5,443 kg) of krill a day!

Most Dangerous Saliva

The Komodo dragon's saliva is poisonous. It can kill a buffalo! First the Komodo dragon bites an animal. Then the saliva goes into the wound and kills the animal. Now the Komodo dragon can eat it!

Komodo Dragon

Very Thirsty Bird

Hummingbirds have long tongues inside their beaks. Their tongues help them feed on sweet nectar from flowers. They can drink up to 14 times their own body weight every day. That would be like a 50-pound (23-kg) seven-year-old drinking two small bathtubs of fruit juice in a day!

Hummingbird

No Tongue

Crabs don't taste with their mouths. They have tiny hairs with taste buds all over their legs and pincers. That means that when a crab touches something, it has already tasted it! Crabs eat plants and animals. They grab tasty fish or shrimp that get too close.

Crab

PROTECT YOUR TONGUE!

It is important to take care of your sense of taste! There are different ways to keep your mouth and your tongue healthy.

It's important to floss before brushing. Floss removes food that gets stuck between teeth.

Brush your teeth twice a day (or more!) to remove bits of food and germs. Make sure to brush your tongue, too!

Be sure to let hot drinks cool so you don't burn your tongue!

Caution
HOT
Beverage

Eat slowly to avoid biting your tongue.

GLOSSARY

mineral (MIN-ur-uhl) a solid substance found in nature that does not come from an animal or plant

nerves (NURVZ) threads that send and receive messages between your brain and other parts of your body so you can move and feel

nutrient (NOO-tree-uhnt) a substance such as a protein, a mineral, or a vitamin that is needed by people, animals, and plants to stay strong and healthy

saliva (suh-LYE-vuh) the watery fluid in your mouth that keeps it moist and helps you soften and swallow food; it also helps kill germs in your mouth

savory (SAY-vur-ee) rich or meaty taste sensation, also called umami

spoiled (SPOILD) rotten or unfit for eating

taste buds (TAYST BUHDZ) groups of cells in the tongue that sense whether something is sweet, sour, salty, bitter, and/or savory

INDEX

ABOUT THE AUTHOR

Claire Caprioli is a children's author. She loves reading, learning, exploring nature, and sharing tasty homemade meals and desserts with her favorite people: her family! You can learn more about her at www.clairecaprioli.com.